NEW VANGUARD • 173

# FRENCH TANKS OF WORLD WAR I

**STEVEN J. ZALOGA**　　　ILLUSTRATED BY TONY BRYAN

First published in Great Britain in 2010 by Osprey Publishing,
Midland House, West Way, Botley, Oxford, OX2 0PH, UK
44–02 23rd St, Suite 219, Long Island City, NY 11101, USA

E-mail: info@ospreypublishing.com

A CIP catalog record for this book is available from the British Library

Print ISBN: 978 1 84603 513 5
E-book ISBN: 978 1 84908 306 5

Page layout by: Melissa Orrom Swan, Oxford
Index by David Worthington
Typeset in Sabon and Myriad Pro
Originated by PPS Grasmere Ltd, Leeds
Printed in China through World Print Ltd.

10 11 12 13 14   10 9 8 7 6 5 4 3 2 1

Osprey Publishing is supporting the Woodland Trust, the UK's leading
woodland conservation charity by funding the dedication of trees.

**www.ospreypublishing.com**

# CONTENTS

# FRENCH TANKS OF WORLD WAR I

## INTRODUCTION

The Renault FT represented the birth of the modern tank, pioneering the classic configuration of a turreted main armament, driver in front, and engine in the rear. This example is seen at a historical re-enactment in France in the 1990s. (Author's collection)

France began developing primitive tanks about the same time as Britain, but introduced them into combat several months later. The two original French tank designs, the St-Chamond and Schneider CA, were seriously flawed and proved to be technical and tactical dead-ends. After a false start, Gen Jean-Baptiste Estienne promoted a more radical idea. Instead of the large and cumbersome tanks then in use with the British and French armies, he proposed building a "bee swarm" of small, inexpensive tanks that could overwhelm the Germans with mobility and mass. The resulting design, the Renault FT, pioneered the classic tank configuration typical of tank designs to this day. It was also the most widely used tank type of World War I, and was the seed for many tank forces after the war including those of the United States and the Soviet Union.

# THE TACTICAL CHALLENGE

After the battlefield turned to stalemate on the Western Front in 1915, the French and British armies studied potential technical solutions to overcome German defensive technology. There were three principal threats that had to be addressed: barbed wire, trenches, and the lethal increase in defensive firepower. These three adversaries were a synergistic combination that shifted the technological and tactical balance back to the defense and led to tactical stalemate. Barbed wire deprived the attacking side of mobility and left the attacking infantry vulnerable to enemy machine-guns. Trenches provided the defender with the means to protect against attacking firepower. The enhanced defensive firepower of 1914–18 made the advancing infantryman vulnerable at greater ranges than ever before. As infantrymen advanced towards enemy lines, they had to endure artillery fire at longer ranges than previously encountered and then, if they survived that, they had to face the murderous scythe of machine-guns and rifle fire.

Early French attempts to develop technical solutions to this tactical dilemma were ingenious but too often focused on one of the threats rather than all three. Armored cars had been adopted by the French cavalry before the war, but these were useless in trench warfare. Their armor did protect against machine-gun fire and against shell splinters, but their narrow wheels created high ground pressure so that they bogged down in soft soil. The primitive automotive suspensions offered no capability to operate in rough terrain. In 1915, the French Army's *Section technique du génie* (STG: Engineer Technical Section) attempted to improve the cross-country mobility of armored cars by building ten armored tractors on Filtz agricultural tractors. These were intended to crush or cut through barbed wire entanglements, but their combat debut at Verdun in the autumn of 1915 demonstrated their arthritic mobility in rough terrain. There were a number of similar schemes during the early years of the war including the armored Archer wheeled tractor, and the Breton-Prétot wire-cutting tractor. Another approach was to use an armored steam-roller as pioneered by the Rouleau Frot-Laffly design of March 1915. The most futuristic designs to deal with barbed wire were the Aubriot-Gabet and Schneider Crocodile land torpedoes,

The Boirault device was the most creative and outlandish of the 1915–16 schemes to develop a machine to overcome barbed wire and trenches. The original version is seen here during trials in 1915. (Author's collection)

This is one of the first production examples of the Schneider CA, pictured at Schneider's Somua plant in St-Ouen. Its main 75mm BS gun can be seen in the right-side swivel mount, with one of its two Hotchkiss machine-guns in a ball mount on the side. (NARA)

also called "*chariots lance-bombes*" ("bomb-throwing vehicles"). These were small, remotely controlled, tracked vehicles which used electric motors that would carry a large explosive charge into the barbed wire entanglements and then blow them up. They never proved reliable or practical enough to be put into production. The most elaborate device to deal with both barbed wire and trenches was the Boirault device nicknamed, appropriately enough, the "*Diplodocus militaris*" ("Military Dinosaur"). The first version of this 30-ton device consisted of a set of hinged frames powered by a motor suspended within the device. Trials in early 1915 failed to convince the French Army of the practicality of the device, so its inventor, Louis Boirault, developed a second design which was smaller and which placed the engine within an armored capsule. After trials in the summer of 1916, Gen Henri Gouraud of the 4th Army found the "*Appareil Boirault no 2*" to be robust and ingenious, but was skeptical of the value of the device due to its size, noise, and vulnerability to German artillery.

The development of the first practical French tanks involved a certain amount of serendipity. In 1914, the armament firm M. M. Schneider & Cie had purchased some American Baby Holt 45hp caterpillar tractors with the hope of adapting them to military requirements beyond their use as artillery tractors. The chief engineer at Schneider's Creusot plant, Eugène Brillié, intended to add an armored superstructure to the tractors along with machine-gun stations and to offer them to the cavalry as tracked assault vehicles. However, this proposal met with disfavor from the politician Jules-Louis Breton, who also served as the Undersecretary of State for Inventions. Breton had been co-inventor of the Breton-Prétot wheeled tractor for cutting barbed wire, and he wanted Schneider to adapt the Baby Holt tractors for this role. While attending a display of the tractors in November 1915, Col Jean-Baptiste Estienne, an artillery commander in Gen Philippe Pétain's 6e *Division d'Infanterie*, realized that the tractors could form the basis for a cross-country combat vehicle. Estienne had a "fervid imagination tempered by common sense" and had already attracted attention in the army for his role in adapting aircraft for artillery spotting. He envisioned the conversion of the tractors into "land battleships" (*cuirasses terrestres*) suitable for knocking out machine-gun nests. They would be armed with a 37mm gun and two machine-guns, have a four-man crew, and be capable of crossing trenches and barbed wire entanglements. In addition, the vehicle would tow an armored trailer carrying 20 infantrymen to support the breakthrough operation. Estienne hoped to accumulate enough support from the field commanders that he could

This interior view of the Schneider CA looking forward shows the Hotchkiss 8mm machine-guns on their pintle mounts and the 75mm BS gun can be seen towards the front right corner. The 75mm ammunition was stowed in the bins behind the gun, as well as in the rear bins in the extreme left of the photo. (NARA)

avoid entanglement with the competing ministries and bureaucracies in Paris. On December 1, 1915, he wrote a letter to the French Army's commander-in-chief, Gen Joseph Joffre, suggesting that his land battleship could be the weapon to relieve the bloody stalemate of trench warfare. As a result, on December 12, 1915, Estienne met with Gen Maurice Janin from Joffre's staff. While Janin expressed considerable interest in the idea, Joffre remained non-committal. However, GQG (*Grand Quartier-Général*: General Headquarters) did give Estienne permission to visit several manufacturers to solicit their interest and aid.

On December 20, 1915, Estienne visited Louis Renault in Paris, but the firm was overwhelmed with war production contracts and showed little enthusiasm for the project. Estienne turned to Schneider and met later in the day with Eugène Brillié. It turned into a fortuitous partnership as Brillié had already been involved in earlier schemes to develop an armored vehicle based on the Baby Holt. Estienne had the vision, combat experience and military connections to push the program with the army; Brillié had the technical knowledge to design the vehicle and the industrial connections to facilitate production.

The nose of the Schneider was shaped like a ship's bow in the vain hope that this would assist in freeing the tank once it made contact with a trench wall. As seen here during the initial training at Marly-le-Roi in 1916, the propulsive power of the vehicle was often insufficient to free its mass in soft ground. (NARA)

After receiving approval from senior corporate officials, Brillié began design studies at the Creusot plant and completed a preliminary design on December 27, 1915, for demonstration to the GQG. By this time, Estienne's former division commander, Gen Pétain, was in the more influential role of commander of the Army of Châlons, and Estienne sought his advice and support for the project. Estienne's proposal won Joffre's support and on February 25, 1916, Schneider received a contract to produce 400 assault vehicles under the cover-name *"Tracteurs Estienne"* with plans to deliver these by November 1916. This program was handed over to one of Schneider's subsidiary facilities, Somua (*Société d'outillage mécanique et d'usinage artillerie*), in St-Ouen on the outskirts of Paris, and the vehicle was designated the Schneider CA (*char d'assaut*)

The production plan went much more slowly than anticipated due to the novelty of the technology, especially the production of armored plate. A full-scale wooden mock-up was built in February and the first prototype was completed in March 1916. The design was based on a lengthened version of the Holt suspension fitted with a rectangular superstructure and a boat-like bow with a Schneider 75mm BS gun in a ball mount on the right side. The 75mm gun was supplemented by two Hotchkiss 8mm machine-guns in swivel mounts on either side. The vehicle had tails at the rear to assist in crossing trenches, and a wire-cutter on the bow.

The first production vehicle was delivered to the Camp de Marly on September 8, 1916. However, by the end of November 1916, when the contract was supposed to have been completed, only eight vehicles had been delivered, of which five had non-hardened steel plate. A total of 32 tanks with mild steel were delivered for training purposes. The program suffered another setback in December 1916 when Gen Robert Nivelle took over army command from Joffre. Nivelle, an artillery officer like Estienne, did not share his enthusiasm for tanks and as a result of his experiences around Verdun, Nivelle wished to place greater emphasis on the production of tractors for towing heavy artillery instead of tanks. As a result, the Schneider program was significantly delayed, with production dragging through 1917.

Besides the production problems, the assault vehicle effort was dealt another blow on September 15, 1916, when the British used their first landships in combat. Estienne had visited Britain in the summer of 1916 to see the British landship designs and to keep the British informed of French

**1. SCHNEIDER CA, CAMP D'ENTRAÎNEMENT DE CHAMPLIEU, APRIL 1917**

The first Schneiders were delivered in artillery gray, but soon were repainted by the *Section Camouflage* detachments in a "flame" pattern of green, brown, and ochre, broken up with black. Tactical markings during the initial training were simple numbers, as seen on this example.

**2. SCHNEIDER CA (*SURBLINDÉ*), AS 2, GROUPEMENT BOSSUT, CHEMIN-DES-DAMES, APRIL 1917**

Prior to the first combat deployment of the Schneiders, a decision was made to adopt standardized tactical insignia based on playing-card symbols in the order Spade (1), Heart (2), Diamond (3) and Club (4), with the symbols representing the four batteries. These were usually applied in white on either side and on the rear. The different groups had variations in this insignia, so AS 2, as seen here, had a hollow circle at the center of the marking; AS 4 had its name below the marking in the format "A4S"; AS 8 had the individual tank number painted under the tactical symbol; AS 9 had the individual tank number painted in the center of the symbol.

The uparmored Schneiders tended to receive a simpler camouflage scheme than the original batch with large patches of ochre, brown and green over the gray, with thick black demarcation lines.

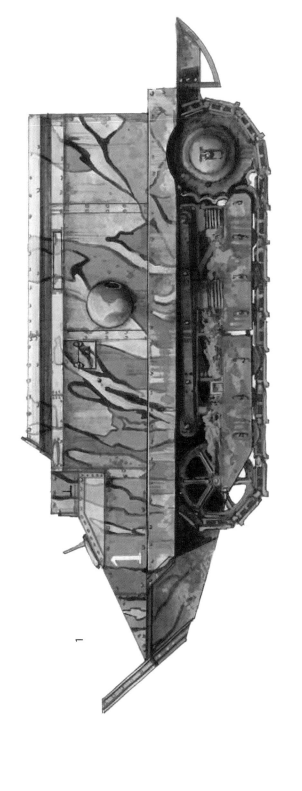

1

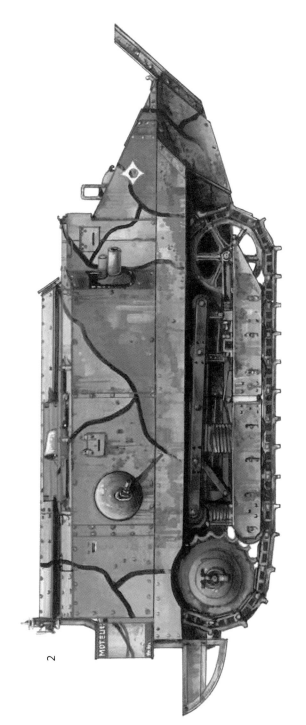

2

The premature combat debut of British tanks prompted the French to reinforce the protection on the Schneiders with spaced armor to defend against German heavy machine-gun fire. This particular tank, 61213, has a somewhat more elaborate version of the *surblindé* kit with a plate on the 75mm BS gun. (NARA)

progress. Estienne made an "earnest and reiterated request" that the British abstain from using their tanks until the French were ready to use theirs to maximize the surprise effect. Joffre had warned the French government that if either the French or British used their vehicles first, the Germans could undermine their tactical value by widening trenches enough to trap assault vehicles in future attacks. The existing Schneider design was limited in its trench-crossing ability to the relatively narrow infantry trenches then in use. However, no formal agreement on this issue was reached though the British Army continued to keep the French appraised of its technical progress if not its planning. Joffre was given a display of the landships on September 3, 1916, but there was no consultation before British commander Gen Sir Douglas Haig deployed the landships on the Somme on September 15, 1916. The premature commitment of the first tanks was criticized by British Prime Minister Lloyd George in his memoirs: "the great secret was sold for a battered ruin of a little hamlet on the Somme not worth capturing." Whether the attack was premature or a necessary experiment with a novel weapon has remained a long-standing controversy between British and French historians of the Great War. Regardless of these arguments, the French carefully studied the lessons of the September 1916 Somme tank debut. Estienne and Joffre presumed that the Germans would quickly respond by deploying small guns in the 37mm range in the forward trenches, widening some trenches to trap the tanks, and deploying mines.

The immediate technical effect on the Schneider assault vehicle was the initiation of a program to increase the frontal armor. The basic frontal armor

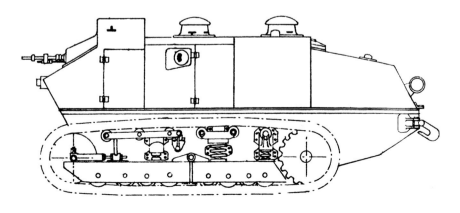

The final version of the Schneider was the CA 3; the S 1058/1059 variant is seen here in the Schneider drawing. This had the engine in the rear and an elongated suspension. Estienne refused to approve the design so the chassis that had already been constructed were used for the manufacture of the Schneider CD artillery tractor.

was 11.5mm thick and an additional 8mm plate was added. This was spaced about 20–40mm away from the basic armor to help defeat improved German machine-gun ammunition. The added armor (*surblindé*) was fitted, starting with Schneider no. 210, at the Somua plant, and kits were dispatched to the main training grounds at Champlieu where they were attached by the local workshops.

## INTO COMBAT

Due to Gen Estienne's prominent role in promoting the assault vehicles, the first French tank units were subordinated to the artillery branch as "*Artillerie Spéciale*" (AS). As a result, the tactical unit organization followed artillery practices. The basic tactical unit was a *groupe* which included four batteries, each with four assault vehicles, and a workshop. During the war, some 17 Schneider groups were formed, numbered AS 1 through AS 17. The French Army was well aware of the maintenance burden that armored vehicles would pose, and so from the outset created a separate supply and repair unit called the SRR (*Section de Ravitaillement et de Réparation*), with the first, S.R.R.101, deployed at Champlieu on December 26, 1916.

Estienne was convinced that the assault vehicles would only be tactically valuable if used *en masse* and so the Schneider groups were hoarded until the next major attack, the Nivelle offensive on the Chemin-des-Dames on April 16, 1917. By this time, 208 Schneider CA had been delivered to the army, of which about 100 were the uparmored CA *surblindé*. Although the original intention had been to use the assault vehicles to create a breakthrough, Estienne was pessimistic about their potential in this role due to German counter-actions since the British tank debut in September 1916. The Germans had widened numerous trenches in the attack sector so the plan required the Schneiders to be used as artillery support weapons that would take over once the infantry had moved beyond the range of divisional artillery and beyond the initial line of German trenches. The changed circumstances after the Somme debut also prompted Estienne to attach pioneer units to the assault vehicle groups to assist in crossing trenches by

The combat debut of French tanks during the Nivelle offensive on the Chemin-des-Dames on April 16, 1917, was extremely disappointing. The *appliqué* armor already added to the baseline Schneider was not sufficient. Here, German troops inspect Schneider No. 61238 commanded by Lt Poupel from the 2e Batterie, AS 2, knocked out east of Juvincourt between the third and fourth German trench line. (NARA)

knocking down trench walls and creating passageways. Eight groups were committed to the Nivelle offensive, totaling 132 Schneider CA. These included *Groupement Bossut* with 82 tanks in five groups (AS 2, 4, 5, 6, 9) supporting the main 32nd Corps attack from Berry-au-Bac between the Aisne and the Miette rivers towards Juvincourt; and *Groupement Chaubès* with 50 tanks in three groups (AS 3, 7, 8) attached to the 5th Corps west of the Miette.

The assault vehicle groups made their approach to the battlefield in columns during daylight and were quickly discovered by German scout aircraft. In many sectors the infantry had failed to create passageways through the forward trenches, which caused considerable delays to the tanks' advance. German artillery was quickly brought into action and proved to be the main cause of tank losses. The only bright spot was a raid by one Schneider group that reached 5km behind German lines. However, it was forced to return due to the lack of infantry support. Of the tanks supporting the 32nd Corps, 31 were knocked out by artillery and 13 broke down or bogged down—more than half the initial force. A total of 129 crewmen were killed or wounded and the *groupement* commander, Commandant Louis Bossut, was among those killed. In the 5th Corps sector, 26 Schneiders, about half the force, were knocked out by artillery; 51 crewmen were casualties. The performance of the Schneiders had been disappointing and the casualties extremely heavy. The Nivelle offensive had failed for more profound reasons than the problems with the Schneiders. The squandering of another 120,000 men so soon after the conclusion of the bloody Verdun fighting was too much for the average *poilu* to bear: his fighting spirit had finally been sapped. The failure of the Nivelle offensive triggered a series of disturbances in the ranks of the army, culminating in the great mutiny of May 3, 1917.

The immediate technical problems of the Schneiders were analyzed and attempts were made to fix the more obvious ones. The worst technical flaw was the forward location of the two fuel tanks. Tanks were most often hit on the front, and artillery penetrations often split open the fuel tanks, spraying the interior with flaming gasoline. This resulted in a program to move the gasoline tanks to the rear of the vehicle where they would be less vulnerable. Two 75-liter tanks were mounted externally on either side of the rear door and this feature was retrofitted to most of the existing fleet. The doors on the Schneider were inadequate for quick crew escape so another door was added on the left side of new-construction tanks. The armor of the Schneider was clearly inadequate,

**B**

### SCHNEIDER CA (*SURBLINDÉ*), 3E BATTERIE, AS 6, AUTUMN 1917

Following the battle on the Chemin-des-Dames, the tankers complained that the Germans had discovered the small view slits and were focusing small-arms fire against them. This could injure or blind the crew since even bullets that did not penetrate would knock off flakes of metal spall near the view slit which would spray into the face and eyes of the crew. As a result, the *Section Camouflage* came up with the novel solution of painting a cross-hatch scheme on the vehicles which would hide the location of the view slits.

Another innovation in 1917 was the development of a means to signal the accompanying infantry. This consisted of a folding metal panel on the roof of the tank that could be lifted vertical from the driver's station by means of a cable. This panel was painted in red with a white stripe to make it clearly visible.

As can be seen, the tactical markings of the groups remained fairly similar to earlier in 1917; in the case of AS 6 the tank number was painted on the tactical symbol with the unit designation painted below.

The early Schneider's greatest weakness was the location of its two fuel tanks in the front of the tank. When hit by artillery fire, the tanks ruptured and sprayed the inside with fuel which then led to catastrophic internal explosions – as occurred here, with tank No. 61216 commanded by Sous-Lieutenant Pierre Desbruères of the 3e Batterie, AS 2. Four of the six men in this tank were killed including the commander, and the other two were wounded. (NARA)

but there was little more that could be done in this regard without making the tank immobile as the Schneider was barely able to traverse the typical battlefield in its current configuration without bogging down. Although the Schneider had been designed with a boat-like bow in the hope that this would facilitate crawling out of a trench or shell-hole, in fact the bow proved ineffective. Estienne had realized this even before the Chemin-des-Dames battles and had requested work on an improved Schneider that would dispense with the bow and so allow the front portion of the tracks to grip the forward obstruction and help lift the tank out. This coincided with another Estienne initiative to create a command tank version with the 75mm gun dropped in favor of a small turreted 47mm gun. A CA 2 prototype was tested at Champlieu in March 1917; it was retired to Marly for training but few records remain. The trials prompted Estienne to promote a new version, with its suspension lengthened by 40cm, sometimes called the CA 3 or CAR 3. Schneider drew up several configurations but Estienne's interest faded due to the lack of an adequate powerplant and the arrival of the Renault FT light tank and its associated specialized variants, as will be described in more detail later.

## AN ELEPHANT ON THE LEGS OF A GAZELLE

The Schneider CA had proven troublesome in its combat debut, but the *Artillerie Spéciale* was about to be saddled with an even more inadequate design. Estienne's unorthodox methods in gaining approval for the construction of the Schneider led to a great deal of resentment in the halls of

**BELOW LEFT**
In the wake of the Nivelle offensive, the Schneiders were modified by removing the internal fuel tanks and shifting them to the rear of the tank on either side of the rear access door. This is the sole surviving example of the Schneider CA 1, displayed for many years at Aberdeen Proving Ground in the United States, but currently preserved at Saumur in France. (Author's Collection)

**BELOW RIGHT**
This is a Schneider CA 1 in the final configuration with the *surblindé* upgrade as well as he rear fuel tanks. (Author's collection)

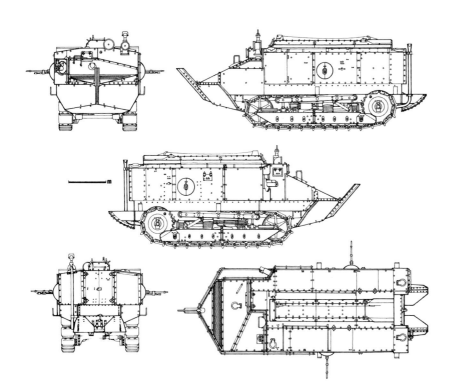

Scale plan of the Schneider CA *surblindé* in the final configuration with the external rear fuel tanks. (Author)

the military–industrial bureaucracy in Paris. This provoked a reaction by the army technical services in Paris, especially the *Direction du Service Automobile* (DSA) under Gen Mourret. Having been upstaged by an upstart artillery colonel, the technical branches in Paris were determined to offer a far grander vehicle than the Schneider. The DSA had been working on an elongated Holt chassis with eight road-wheels per side versus six on the Schneider and a crude mockup of the *cuirassé terrestre* sponsored by Mourret was demonstrated in March 1916. If the Schneider were armed with a short 75mm gun, then the new rival tank would have a long 75mm field gun; if the Schneider had two machine-guns, then the new tank would have four. On paper, the new *char d'assaut* St-Chamond was much more impressive than the smaller Schneider. However, it had been designed by engineers with no appreciation of trench warfare.

After further scheming with the various ministries, a contract for 400 "supplementary" tanks was awarded to the FAMH steelworks (*Forges et aciéries de la marine et d'Homécourt*) in St-Chamond. One of the most curious but questionable technical innovations of the tank was the decision to use a Crochat-Collardeau electrical powertrain. Instead of the 80hp Panhard engine powering a conventional mechanical transmission, the engine powered a 52 kilowatt electrical generator which fed power to a pair of separate electric motors for the drive sprocket on either side of the tank. This eliminated the usual gearbox and made it much easier to steer the tank compared with the braking system used on the Schneider, but the innovation came at the price of considerably greater complexity and costs. Development of the St-Chamond tank at FAMH was directed by the retired colonel Émile Rimailho, a well-known French artillery designer. The tank was armed with a gun of Rimailho's design, the St-Chamond 75mm TR (*tir rapide*: rapid fire).

The St-Chamond tank was significantly longer than the Schneider with a protruding bow. One scheme was to mount a small tracked bogie under the nose to facilitate crawling out of trenches, but in the end a set of rollers was fitted under the nose as a simpler solution. As well as this problem, the first prototype demonstrated in the autumn of 1916 showed a tendency to bog down due to the narrow track and the vehicle's heavy weight. The track width was increased three times from 324mm to 412mm and finally to 500mm in the final production batch. Other problems included fuel flow interruption when the tank was inclined, deformation of the suspension bogies, and poor ventilation inside the tank. The mechanical problems with the St-Chamond, and especially the weak powertrain, led one observer to deride it as "an elephant on the legs of a gazelle."

Even before the St-Chamond had entered service, the army wanted improvements. At a meeting on January 18, 1917, representatives from the army's *Section Techniques Automobiles* met with Col Rimailho and other factory officials to discuss future plans. There was a clear need for a tracked vehicle for the SRR to use to conduct recovery and supply operations, and so 48 tanks were to be set aside from the 400-tank production contract. The "*chars caissons*" were essentially the same as the cannon-armed tanks, but with the gun and machine-gun apertures plated over. There were complaints that the fighting compartment roof was too low for efficient crew operations and that the flat roof would be vulnerable to grenades and satchel charges thrown by the German infantry. As a result, vehicles after No. 150 (military serial number 62550) were to be built in a new configuration with a pitched roof. There were plans to substitute the Schneider 75mm M12 for the St-Chamond 75mm TR on tanks No. 151 to 210, but enough 75mm TR were available that tanks in the intermediate series retained the original gun.

### 1. ST-CHAMOND, 2E BATTERIE, AS 31, LAFFAUX, MAY 5, 1917

The *Section Camouflage* detachment that painted the tanks of AS 31 and other groups of this *groupement* came up with one of the most elaborate schemes used during the war, consisting of a complex pattern of colors over the base artillery gray color. Patches of black were used extensively to hide the view slits and machine-gun ports, and a *trompe d'oeil* was employed in the form of a false machine-gun port painted on the rear hull side. Tanks in this unit had names painted in large and elaborate letters, sometimes accompanied by a cartoon – in this case the "singing Rooster" (*Chantecoq*).

### 2. ST-CHAMOND, AS 35, AUTUMN 1917

The AS 35 also enjoyed a fairly elaborate color scheme of waves of ochre, brown and green over the base gray color with patterns of black to break up the colors. This particular tank carried not only the name "Tintine" on the gun barrel and an elaborate unit crest, but also a marking of a horseshoe with Caesar's Latin slogan "Veni, Vidi, Vici" ("I came, I saw, I conquered") and the name "stella" inside.

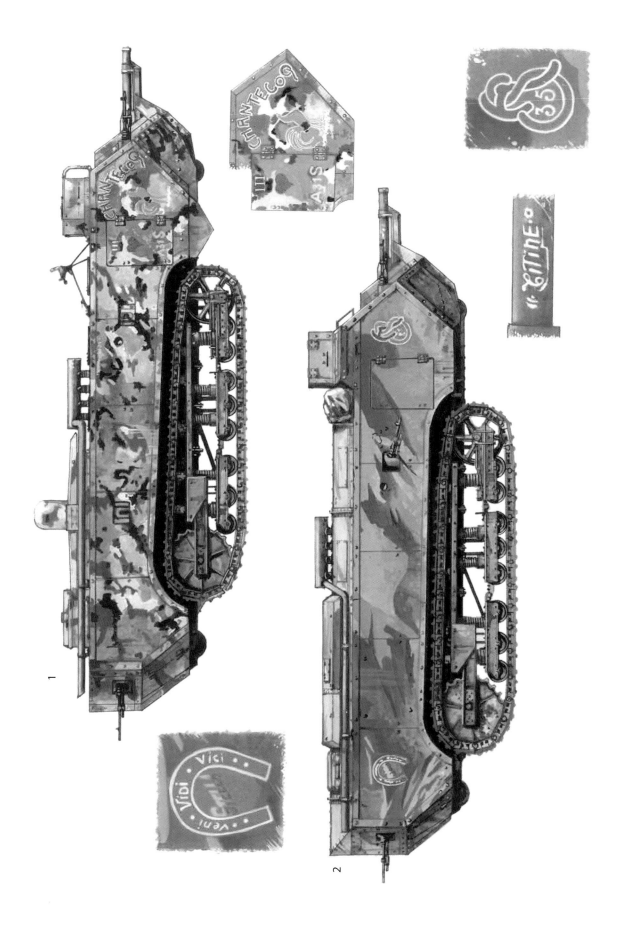

In the end, 60 tanks were built in this configuration – serial numbers 62551 to 62610. Gen Mourret insisted that the St-Chamond eventually be re-armed with the more common 75mm M1897, starting with tank No. 211. A total of 190 tanks were eventually built with the M1897, serials 62611 to 62800. Although not discussed at this time, when the intermediate production St-Chamond entered service it was quickly realized that the deletion of the roof cupolas for the driver had been a mistake, and so the final production run of the St-Chamond had a rectangular cupola added.

This photo aptly illustrates two of the problems with the initial production configuration of the St-Chamond. The flat roof not only restricted the space inside the fighting compartment, but was a tempting target for German infantry to throw grenades or satchel charges at. Although grenades could not penetrate the armor, their detonation could knock off spall from the inner face of the armor. The tendency of the St-Chamond to ditch itself is all too evident in this view. (NARA)

In spite of the tank's problems, the first St-Chamond group, AS 31, was formed at Champlieu in late February 1917. The original scheme had been to deploy mixed groups with Section A consisting of two batteries of Schneiders and Section B having two batteries of the St-Chamond. However, the delay in manufacturing the St-Chamond led to the formation of homogenous groups. Although there were about 30 St-Chamonds on hand in April 1917 at the time of the Nivelle offensive, none were committed to combat as too many of the tanks still had the original narrow tracks which were unsuitable for use on soft ground. Due to their machines' greater size, the St-Chamond groups had fewer tanks than the Schneider groups – only three batteries with four tanks each.

The combat debut of the St-Chamond was delayed until May 5, 1917, when it took part in a minor attack near Laffaux Mill which involved two Schneider groups and one St-Chamond group. The St-Chamond suffered significant problems with mobility and mechanical breakdowns, but the attack was a mixed success with the Germans crediting the French tanks with destroying many machine-gun nests and assisting the infantry advance. Losses were three St-Chamonds and three Schneiders.

The next major French offensive was delayed after Gen Phillipe Pétain replaced the disgraced Nivelle on May 15, 1917. Pétain was very different from previous commanders-in-chief. Unlike most French officers of the time, he was no disciple of the Grandmaison school and the obsession with offensive tactics and the mythical *élan vitale* of the French soldier epitomised by the mindless slogan "*L'audace, l'audace, toujours l'audace*" ("Boldness, boldness, always boldness"). His tour of command during the Verdun fighting had

"Fantomas", a colorfully marked St-Chamond of the initial production series, served in AS 31 before being knocked out in combat. (Pierre Touzin)

convinced him of the bankruptcy of Grandmaison's influences. To Pétain, a more appropriate slogan for the nature of tactics in the age of the machine-gun was "firepower kills." Appalled by the callousness shown by many staff officers towards the massive losses of infantrymen, he searched for new tactics to overcome the dominance of defensive machine-gun and artillery fire.

Pétain quickly appreciated that the new tanks, even if they did not live up to the extravagant claims of their advocates like Estienne, were very important morale-boosters for the disheartened infantry. As the French Minister of Munitions later quipped: "There are two kinds of infantry; men who have gone into action with tanks, and men who have not; and the former never want to go into action without tanks again." Pétain was not overly concerned about Estienne's promises that tanks would provide the key breakthrough weapon: he viewed them as the glue to hold together his disheartened troops, and a means to help revive their fighting spirit.

Pétain also saw that the full potential of the tanks would not be realized unless there was better tank–infantry cooperation. As a result, the first major offensive since the mutinies around Malmaison on October 23, 1917, was preceded by intense tank–infantry training. The attack included 36 Schneider and 56 St-Chamond tanks of which only two were lost. In addition to the improved tank–infantry cooperation, the foggy conditions aided the French attack and made it much more difficult for the German artillerymen to see the attacking French tanks. The German infantrymen were very disheartened to see their SmK armor-piercing machine-gun rounds bounce harmlessly off the Schneider CA *surblindé*. Malmaison was the first success for the French tank

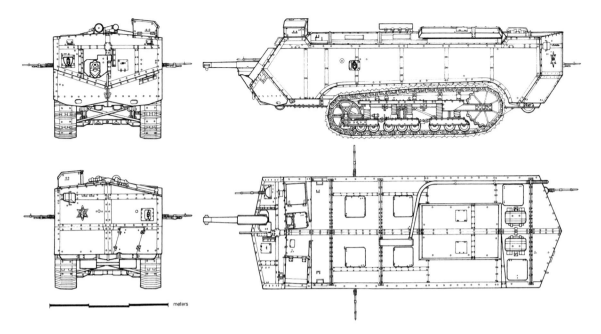

Scale plan of the final production version of the St-Chamond with the 75mm M1897 gun. (Author)

force, and even though this was an action of modest scale, it encouraged the further expansion of the *Artillerie Spéciale*. One technical innovation adopted in October 1917 was the conversion of two Schneider and two St-Chamond tanks into *"chars TSF"* (*télégraphie sans fils*: wireless radio) in order to provide a means of communication between the tank groups and the infantry division headquarters they were supporting.

## THE LIGHT TANK IDEA

Following the construction of the first Schneiders in the spring of 1916, Estienne began considering long-term requirements for the *Artillerie Spéciale*. Construction of the Schneider had made Estienne aware of the industrial road-blocks to building a vast fleet of armoured vehicles with which to overwhelm the German trenches. French military factories were in a desperate state: the mass mobilization of skilled manpower in 1914 and the horrendous

A total of 48 St-Chamond tanks were diverted to serve as *"chars caissons"* which were used for tank recovery and bringing supplies to the front. They were identical to the tank version, but had their guns removed and the forward embrasure plated over. This example is based on the initial series with the flat roof and is seen here near Cutrey on June 16, 1918, while supporting the 1st Division of the American Expeditionary Force (AEF). (NARA)

The initial production series of 150 Renault FT were *"chars d'instruction"* constructed of soft steel. They used this distinctive turret which was enlarged on the production version for better ventilation. The army *matricule* 66040 suggests that this is the 40th tank built from the November 1917 batch. This particular example was one of the tanks handed over to the AEF for training at the Langres center in 1918. (NARA)

loss of life in the first two years of the war had left the factories short of skilled workers. Armor plate was at a premium, as were high-powered engines. The Schneider facilities were overtaxed producing their first 400 tanks, which were not completed until 1918. What was needed was a small, cheap armored machine-gun vehicle, tailored to the limitations of the French wartime industries. In July 1916, Estienne raised the issue with the auto manufacturer Louis Renault at a chance meeting in the Hotel Claridge. Renault had earlier refused to become involved in the medium tank program, citing his firm's lack of experience with tracked vehicles and commitments to other programs. However, Renault was intrigued by the light tank idea, and agreed to begin design studies of such a vehicle under the direction of one of his engineers, Charles-Edmond Serre. The new vehicle was called a *char mitrailleur* (machine-gun vehicle).

A wooden mock-up of the *char mitrailleur* was completed in October 1916 and shown to Estienne. He could not persuade Gen Mourret of the DSA to authorize production so, on 27 November, 1916, went over Mourret's head to Gen Joffre, the commander-in-chief. Joffre supported his request for 1,000 of these vehicles and on November 30, 1916 wrote to the Under-Secretary of State for War, Albert Thomas, on this subject. Thomas was only willing to allow the construction of a single prototype as he was not very enthused by the project and was one of the backers of the DSA's St-Chamond project. His obstructiveness over the next few months considerably delayed the program. On December 30, 1916, Renault showed a refined, full-scale wooden mock-up to the Consultative Committee of the Assault Artillery. Gen Mourret felt that the tank's center of gravity was too far to the rear and the tank too light; another member suggested that ventilation was inadequate and would result in the asphyxiation of the crew after ten minutes of firing. One officer complimented the elegance of the design but sarcastically referred to it as a *"charmant joujou"* ("a charming toy") of little combat utility. However, the remainder of the committee did not agree, and on the basis of a seven-to-three vote, the committee accepted the design and approved the production of an initial batch of 100 *chars mitrailleurs*.

This vehicle soon became labeled the Renault FT. There is some confusion as to the origin of the designation "FT" for this tank. It has been incorrectly described as an abbreviation for *faible tonnage* (light weight) or *franchisseur des tranchées* (trench-crosser). In fact, however, it was simply a Renault

**ABOVE LEFT**
The small cast turret found on the original *char d'instruction* was replaced by the enlarged Berliet "omnibus" turret which could be fitted with either a 37mm gun or an 8mm Hotchkiss machine-gun, as seen here. The rigid frame for the suspension bogies resulted in a rough ride for the Renault FT crew when cresting any appreciable incline in the terrain. This is a Renault-built tank, factory serial number 919 and army *matricule* 66160. (NARA)

**ABOVE RIGHT**
The Berliet riveted omnibus turret Renault FT could also be fitted with a Puteaux 37mm gun as a *char canon*. (NARA)

product designation given in sequential order to all Renault automobiles and vehicles, such as the AG (Marne taxi), the EG (artillery tractor), the FU (heavy lorry), etc. Officially, it became known as the *char léger Renault FT modèle 1917*, which has sometimes led to the unofficial abbreviation "FT-17".

The 100-tank order of December 1916 was amended in February 1917 to 150 tanks. The first *char mitrailleur* prototype was completed at the end of January 1917, and put through tests at the Renault factory at Billancourt.

**French tank camouflage: the "*Camoufleurs*"**
The French Army pioneered the use of pattern-painted camouflage in World War I. At the start of the war, most heavy equipment was painted in overall *gris artillerie* (artillery gray), a pre-war choice based in some measure on the availability of anti-rust zinc industrial paint. Some equipment was also painted in more expensive *vert armée* (army green), a dark olive green. Since tanks were part of the artillery, the first tanks were painted in artillery gray when delivered from the factories, but this was quickly overpainted with garish camouflage colors. French interest in camouflage painting had been inspired by Guirand de Scevola, an academic painter who was serving in an artillery regiment near Metz early in the war. De Scevola was well versed in various artistic theories about human visual perception, especially Cubism, and persuaded his unit's officers to let him try disguising the unit's gun batteries. This effort was so successful that on February 12, 1915, the Ministry of War established the "*Section Camouflage*" under De Scevola which set about recruiting artists and craftsmen to assist in camouflage efforts. Although these efforts largely involved the development of camouflage nets and other forms of camouflage materials, De Scevola and other artists came up with elaborate schemes to camouflage-paint artillery to break up the guns' distinctive shapes. These patterns were dubbed "*zébrage*", better known as dazzle-painting in Britain. First applied to artillery and later to tanks, the camouflage was intended to confuse the viewer regarding the actual shape and details of the object more than to blend it into the background. The early camouflage schemes tended to be quite intricate and fussy, involving multiple paint colors which required considerable skill to apply. By late 1917, this gave way to simpler patterns that could be applied by minimally skilled workers in factories or depots. Studies conducted by the air force in 1917 led to the abandonment of the pre-war artillery gray color as it was found to be too evident on aerial photographs. The preferred color was a dull, dark green-brown, the precursor of the olive drab and olive green shades so widely used ever since on tanks.

Estienne had the prototype sent to the *Artillerie Spéciale* center at Champlieu for further tests to correct any remaining problems; he was aware that recent political changes could doom his project, and he was insistent that the *char mitrailleur* should be perfected before its official trials in April.

## BUREAUCRATIC DELAYS

In the wake of the horrible blood-letting around Verdun, Gen Joffre was sacked on December 13, 1916, and replaced by Gen Robert Nivelle. Estienne lost his protector, and Gen Mourret continued to make known his lack of enthusiasm for the cheap little Renault *char mitrailleur*. As mentioned earlier, Nivelle was not fond of the tank idea and wanted the scarce factory resources directed towards artillery tractors instead. As a result the Minister of Armaments, Albert Thomas, informed Renault that priority was to be given to the completion of an existing contract for artillery tractors at the expense of the tank program. Thomas was very unhappy with Estienne's proposal to build 1,000 of the Renault *char mitrailleur*, feeling this would completely disrupt the already overtaxed French war industry. However, the Consultative Committee of the Assault Artillery supported Estienne enthusiastically, and on 10 April voted for the production of 1,000 more Renault FT tanks. The committee even managed to win over Gen Nivelle, who reversed his earlier decision on April 13, 1917, now giving priority to tank production. The official trials of the prototype were conducted at Marly on April 21–22, 1917. The Renault vehicle was judged clearly superior to the existing Schneider and St-Chamond tanks. Estienne suggested that some of the tanks might be fitted with a small 37mm gun derived from the 37mm modèle 16 TR infantry gun. This would require redesign of the turret. Several committee members felt that the accommodation for the machine-gunner was too small and cramped – it would be difficult for a soldier over 5ft 6in. tall to operate in the turret – and would lead to asphyxiation.

On 29 April, 1917, Thomas received news of some of the criticisms of the Renault FT from disgruntled opponents of the project, and used this as an excuse to suspend the planned production yet again. He claimed that a single soldier could not operate the turret weapon; but his suggestion that another man be added to the turret implied prolonged delays while the tank was completely redesigned. He had also heard that some observers wanted the tank to carry 10,000 rounds of machine-gun ammunition instead of the 1,820 allowed in the current design!

**Key**

1  Clutch pedal
2  Left turn brake lever
3  Brake pedal
4  Right turn brake lever
5  Engine clutch gear lever
6  Driver access hatch latch
7  Driver's armored visor (open)
8  Puteaux 37mm gun
9  Telescopic sight for gun
10 Commander's ventilation dome/cupola cover
11 Right hull side 37mm ammunition stowage

12 Fuel hatch
13 Fuel tank
14 Radiator water hatch
15 Muffler
16 Armored cover over engine air vent
17 Tank tarp
18 Unditching tail
19 Engine
20 Engine radiator

21 Transmission
22 Drive sprocket
23 Left hull side 37mm ammunition stowage
24 Driver instruments
25 Driver seat
26 Spring for return roller race
27 Front idler wheel

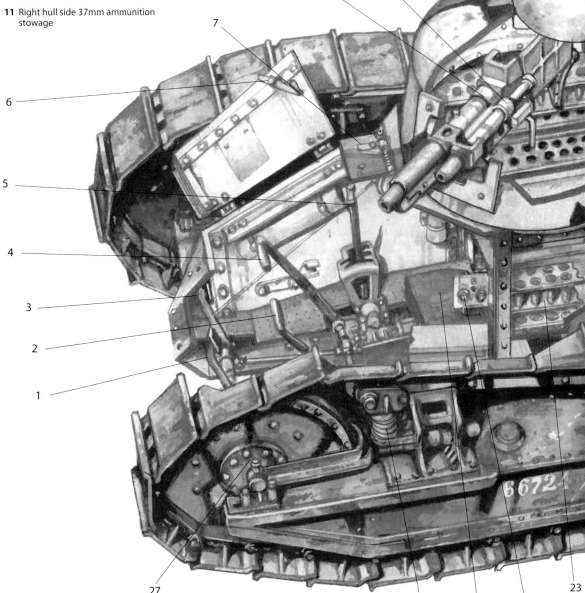

**Technical data**

**Crew** 2 (commander/gunner and driver)

**Weight** 6.48 metric tons (14,300lb)

**Length** 5m (16ft 5in)

**Width** 1.74m (5ft 7in)

**Height** 2.14m (7ft)

**Armor** Hull front 16mm, sides 8mm, cast turret 22mm, riveted turret 16mm

**Engine** Renault 18CV, 35hp

**Fuel** 57 liters (22gal)

**Maximum speed** 7.5km/h (4.8mph)

**Trench crossing** 1.8m (6ft)

**Vertical obstacle** 0.65m (2ft)

**Range** 35km (25mi)

**Armament** Puteaux 37mm SA modèle 18 gun or Hotchkiss 8mm modèle 1914 machine-gun

**Ammunition** 237 37mm rounds or 4,800 8mm rounds

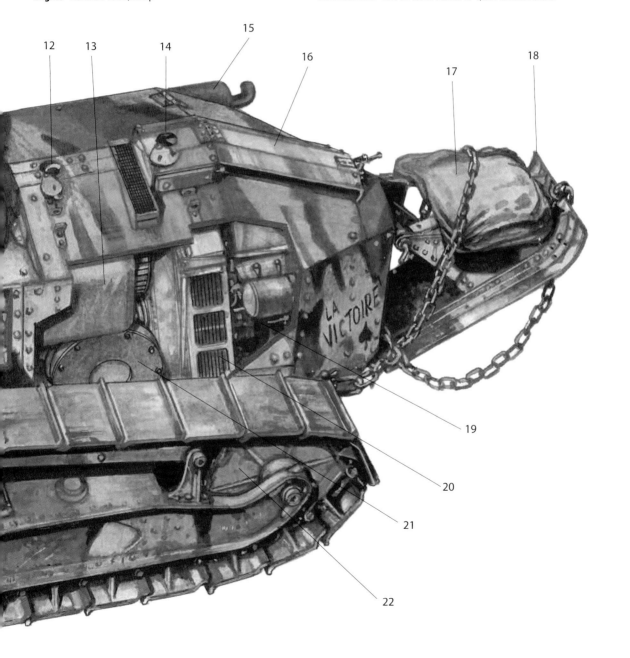

Estienne and Renault – whose firm was already gearing up to produce the tank – were furious over the decision. During the course of the trials the Nivelle offensive had been launched on the Chemin-des-Dames, and it was an utter failure. Estienne was even more convinced of the need for masses of light tanks to overcome the trench-war stalemate. Thomas, a prominent socialist and a correspondent for *L'Humanité*, was invited to Russia to celebrate the overthrow of the Tsar and the accession to power of Kerensky's socialist provisional government. While Thomas was out of France, Estienne staged another series of trials for the benefit of a number of officers who had fought on the Chemin-des-Dames during the first French tank actions on April 16, 1917. Their enthusiastic reaction to the Renault FT convinced even Gen Mourret that the tank had reached a sufficient stage of development for production, and Thomas' orders were again revoked. It was also decided that of the 1,150 tanks on order, 650 would be armed with the new 37mm gun and 500 with the 8mm Hotchkiss machine-gun. By the time that Thomas returned to France, repercussions from the Nivelle offensive prevented his further interference in the Renault FT tank program.

## PÉTAIN'S REFORMS

As described earlier, Nivelle staged his ill-fated offensive on the Chemin-des-Dames on April 16, 1917, and this included the first use of French tanks. The mutiny on May 3, 1917, incapacitated the French Army through most of the summer and led to a profound reconsideration of French tactics by its new chief, Gen Philippe Pétain. Estienne had served as an artillery regiment commander in Pétain's division in 1914 and they had a number of conversations during the summer of 1917. Pétain listened with interest to Estienne's new ideas, like the "bee theory." Estienne argued that the loss of surprise after the British use of tanks in 1916 meant that tanks would inevitably be confronted by artillery. The Schneider and St-Chamond tanks were too thinly armoured and too big to survive in a duel with artillery; no tank could be constructed which would resist the standard German 77mm field gun. Instead of confronting German defenses with impregnable armour, they could be confronted with mass instead. Five little Renault FTs could be built for every heavy tank – five little "bee" tanks with five machine-guns or cannon were better than a single big St-Chamond with one gun and five machine-guns, and far less vulnerable. The FTs would be much more difficult targets due to their small size, and a "bee swarm" of FTs would overcome the small number of German guns by weight of numbers. Pétain heartily endorsed this notion, and on June 20 decided to increase the number of FTs ordered from 1,150 to 3,500 at the expense of proposed new medium tanks; he viewed this as an essential factor in his efforts to restore the French Army. He made his troops a promise: there would be no major offensives until the Americans and the new tanks arrived. The new Renault FT tanks would be held back until enough were ready for a massive offensive in the spring of 1918.

The many delays and bureaucratic obstacles to Renault FT production were reduced by Pétain's arrival. After further arguments with Pétain, Thomas was relieved as Minister of Armaments in September 1917, and his place was taken by Louis Loucheur. Renault proved unable to cope with the expanding number of orders, and so Louis Renault agreed to waive any production patents and encouraged the ministry to extend production to other factories. These eventually included Berliet, Schneider's Somua facility and Delaunay-Belleville. In addition, it was proposed to include American and later Italian factories. Plans and a single tank were dispatched to the US in September 1917 with the aim of producing 1,200 more Renault FT tanks for the French Army as well as sufficient tanks for the US Army. As of December 1, 1917, the total production order was expanded to 3,100 tanks (1,950 with the 37mm gun and 1,150 with the machine-gun); 700 support tanks with a 75mm BS short howitzer; and 200 TSF radio tanks. On February 17, 1918, the totals were again revised, to 1,000 machine-gun tanks, 1,830 37mm gun tanks, 200 TSF radio tanks, and 970 tanks with 75mm BS howitzer or other types to be decided. By October 1918 the total orders had been raised to an astounding 7,820 tanks in France alone. The factory breakdown was as follows (October 1918 orders in parentheses):

A Renault FT *char mitrailleur* with the Girod turret at the Langres tank school on July 15, 1918.

1,850 (3,940) tanks from Renault, 800 (1,995) from Berliet, 600 (1,135) from Somua, and 280 (750) from Delaunay-Belleville.

In 1917 Renault produced only 84 tanks, which was considerably behind schedule. One of the main design problems was the turret. A small cast turret was used on the first production run of training tanks, but it was widely regarded as being too small. A second cast-turret design was stillborn as by the time it was ready, Estienne wanted it to mount either a 37mm gun or a machine-gun and it was only capable of mounting the latter. In addition, there were limits to the number of cast turrets that could be manufactured. In the end, Berliet developed a simpler polygonal turret made of sheet armor plate, called the omnibus turret. The advantage of the omnibus turret was that it could be adapted to mount either the 37mm Puteaux gun, or the 8mm Hotchkiss machine-gun. Eventually, a second, round omnibus turret was also developed. This was manufactured at the Aciéries Paul Girod in Ugine from cast and forged pieces. Girod began producing round omnibus turrets in 1918, and the tanks built at Renault in 1918 used both types of turret. Girod also supplied the round turret to the other FT manufacturers.

Deliveries of the first Renault FT *char léger* (light tank) were further delayed by problems in the supply of armor plate, some of which came from Britain, and in the supply of armament, especially the new 37mm gun. Nearly three-quarters of the first tanks were found to have serious defects; often, these had to be returned to the factory for correction. There was a serious shortage of spare parts, especially at unit level. Many of the first units were hobbled due to two seemingly minor problems: the poor quality of the fuel filters and the fan-belts. For example, in July 1918 ten percent of the tanks in the 503e Regiment were immobilized due to broken fan-belts. Both problems continued to plague the Renault tank until the end of the war.

By February 1918 there were still only 108 Renaults at the main training ground at Champlieu, and none had armament. By the beginning of April some 453 tanks had been delivered from the factories, of which 43 were combat-ready, 122 were unarmed and being used for training and 248 were sitting at Chalais-Meudon waiting for army acceptance testing. The first light

World War I tanks were not very durable, so French units quickly learned the value of moving them to the front line using either railroads or trucks. The Renault FT was small enough that it could be moved using trucks, as seen here in 1918. (Pierre Touzin)

tank battalion, the 1e BCL (*Battalion des chars légers*) was formed, without complete equipment, on February 18, 1918. On March 21, it received a full complement of 75 tanks, but without armament. Two more companies were formed in March, but without tanks.

## RENAULT UNIT ORGANIZATION

The Renault FT units were organized in a fundamentally different fashion from those of the earlier medium tanks. They were formed into larger tank battalions consisting of three tank companies, numbering 75 tanks at full strength. The original plans called for a battalion to include 30 gun tanks, 41 machine-gun tanks and 4 radio tanks; this mixture was seldom achieved in practice. The radio tanks did not begin arriving until July, and there was a shortage of machine-gun tanks. The tank companies had a headquarters (one radio tank in theory, a gun tank in practice); three sections with five tanks (three gun tanks, two machine-gun tanks); a reserve echelon with five replacement tanks; a supply and recovery section with three tanks (two gun, one machine-gun); a company workshop and a transport detachment. Later, the companies were issued no reserve tanks, and a battalion reserve of about 25 tanks was retained under central control; these were sometimes used to form a provisional company during the fighting. The nominal organization of the tank units quickly fell apart in combat due to the high level of attrition. It was not unusual for a unit to lose half its strength in a single day of fighting mainly due to mechanical breakdowns and ditching, and its strength and the state of its equipment would vary wildly as tanks were recovered and brought back into action over the subsequent days. In May 1918, the army decided to create larger formations, the RAS (*Régiments d'Artillerie Spéciales*) which included three light tank battalions plus the support elements. The first of these was the 501e RAS which included the 1e, 2e, and 3e BCL. The companies within these were numbered sequentially so 1e BCL had the AS 301, 302 and 303.

French tank battalions had a fourth "echelon" company which served as a reserve and helped move supplies. Here, the 17e BCL, 506e RAS, is seen on trains near Vadelaincourt on September 25, 1918. Behind the nearest tank is a stack of wooden sledges, used by the echelon tanks to tow fuel and ammunition. (NARA)

## FACING THE CHALLENGE

It had been the dream of all the tank advocates, both British and French, to be able to hoard their tanks for one grand onslaught against the German lines. Estienne had prevailed on Pétain to build up a large force of Renaults before putting them into action. Pétain had planned to wait until a strike force of 12 battalions (864 tanks) was built up before committing the Renault FT to combat. However, with all the delays, the expectations were whittled down to six battalions, totaling 432 tanks, for May 1, 1918. This was not to be.

On March 21, 1918, the German Army launched its great Ludendorff "peace offensive" on the Western Front, and the Germans were soon on the doorstep of the main French tank base at Champlieu. The first 37mm guns were not delivered to the 1e and 2e BCL until the night of March 23–24. The German offensive forced the abandonment of Champlieu, and severely disrupted the process of organizing and training the first FT units. The month of April was spent trying to get the first three battalions fully equipped and ready for combat.

The first unit committed to action was the 501e RAS, numbering about 200 Renault FT tanks. It supported Gen Mangin's six infantry divisions in an attempt to stave off German attacks towards the Fôret de Retz on the approaches to Paris. The three battalions were broken up into small groups of 30 or so tanks to support specific infantry attacks. On May 31, 1918, the first Renaults entered combat alongside Moroccan infantry around Ploissy-Chazelle. For the next two weeks the Renaults were used in a series of small local attacks and counter-attacks, sometimes in the dense undergrowth of the forest itself.

The Renaults proved their worth immediately. Their smaller size and the rotating gun turret permitted their use in forested areas where the French medium tanks or British rhomboids would have been nearly useless. The forested areas were traversed by narrow tracks which would have stopped vehicles any larger. The tanks' presence bolstered the French infantry, even if co-operation between tanks and footsoldiers was almost uniformly poor. In more open terrain, the tanks were usually able to overcome frontline German machine-gun nests and install the *poilus* in the new positions. However, there were never enough Renaults; nor did the French infantry hold terrain the way they did in 1915 or 1916. The small Renault units quickly became exhausted in terms of both men and machines due to the clamor for their support.

A pair of Renault FT *char canon* of the AEF 326th Battalion move forward near Boureuilles supporting the 35th Division on September 26, 1918. The lead tank is fitted with the Girod turret while the second tank has a riveted omnibus turret.

A French Renault FT *char mitrailleur* of the 5e BCL, 502e RAS near Juvigny on August 29, 1918, while supporting the AEF's 32nd Infantry. (NARA).

The Renault tank had proven itself from a technical standpoint. It was highly regarded by the troops, and its performance in sustained operations with minimal technical support was miraculous by Great War standards. Its impact on the course of the battle was minimized by its use in very small numbers and the fact that the infantry were unaccustomed to working alongside tanks.

By early June 1918, the force of Schneiders and St-Chamonds had risen to its wartime peak with nearly 500 in service. To better mass these forces, the company-size groups had been consolidated into eight *groupements* (regiments); the Schneider *groupements* were numbered I to IV and the St-Chamond X to XIII. These had a nominal strength of four groups and a total of 64 tanks each, though the actual strength in the field was less. Aside from some small actions and the employment of AS 5 to support the AEF near Cantigny on May 28, the heavy tanks were held in reserve. The Ludendorff offensive reached its high-water mark in June on the approaches to Paris, and Gen Mangin built up a counter-attack force with 163 medium tanks in four *groupements*. The French tanks attacked on June 11 in the Matz valley with a total of 51 Schneider and 96 St-Chamond tanks, losing 35 Schneiders and 37 St-Chamond tanks. Groupement III lost nearly 70% of its Schneiders and Groupement X lost nearly 80% of its St-Chamonds in the intense fighting. In spite of the heavy losses, the tank attacks helped blunt the German offensive.

On July 18, 1918, the French Army began its offensive near Soissons, which saw the largest commitment of French armor to date, including 255 Renaults, 100 St-Chamonds and 123 Schneiders. The little Renaults were the vanguards of the attack. After passing the first waves of infantry, it was often the Renaults that provided the impetus for the advance. They were the critical ingredient in determining how far and how fast local attacks would penetrate. The advances were often halted only by the lack of fresh infantry to hold on to the terrain seized by the tanks, or to continue to press the attack forward. The Soissons offensive showed the offensive power of tanks, and led to enthusiastic calls from the French infantry commanders who had previously been unenthusiastic. The Soissons attack was the swan-song of the medium tanks due to the heavy attrition of the June–July fighting and the end of

The small size of the Renault FT made it vulnerable to a host of threats. This destroyed Renault FT has a large gash in the forward floor, suggesting that it struck a large German mine that blew it in half. (NARA)

medium tank production. The Renault FT began to play the dominant role in French tank actions, with new battalions being added at a rate of almost one per week.

The most significant tactical problem was the continued lack of sufficient tank–infantry training. The tank units had trouble enough bringing their units up to full strength, with never enough time – or enough tanks – to practice tank–infantry co-operation. Every single operational tank was hoarded for combat use, since training led to rapid mechanical deterioration. The tanks were good for only a few dozen hours of operation before they required an overhaul. Tank–infantry training usually only occurred on the battlefield itself. Few infantry units showed any skill in operating with tanks until their second battle. An American officer later wrote of the Renault tank units: "Given seasoned divisions trained with and assisted by tanks, nothing can stop them."

The appearance of large numbers of tanks in the summer fighting heralded the end of the hegemony of the machine-gun on the battlefield. The growing effectiveness and numbers of the French tank units in the summer 1918 fighting led to a number of German attempts to develop tactical improvements to deal with them. One German response was to begin to fortify machine-guns in small concrete pillboxes. These began to appear in large numbers in the late summer of 1918. They made it more difficult and costly for the Renaults to overcome the machine-guns, since it was usually necessary for a gun-armed FT to approach close enough to fire directly into the gun slit. At such close ranges, the German machine-gunners were trained to fire at the vision slits on the Renault. The bullets would not penetrate the Renault's thick frontal armour, but spall knocked off near the point of impact on the inside of the tank could injure or blind the crew. The pillboxes were an inadequate response to the growing number of Renaults, since the more fluid conditions of the battlefield in the autumn of 1918 made it more difficult to establish elaborate static defense lines. The German Army

**E**   **ST-CHAMOND, AS 31, BATTLE OF MALMAISON, OCTOBER 23, 1918**
The tank, named Yvette, was commanded by Adjutant Moreau of the 4e Batterie, AS 31, during the autumn fighting. Like other tanks of the *groupe*, it is painted in a particularly elaborate camouflage scheme.

began to appreciate that a more satisfactory response would be the fielding of a counterpart to the Renault to act as a mobile, protected machine-gun nest. However, the German LK light tank was not ready for mass production in 1918.

German field guns remained the principal threat to French tanks; of the 440 Renaults lost during the war, 356 were lost to artillery. French tactics stressed the need for artillery-fired smoke rounds to prevent enemy gunners from engaging the tanks at long ranges. However, close co-operation with the French artillery was difficult to achieve in an era before reliable radios. The main advantage that the Renaults enjoyed over earlier French or British tanks was their small size and greater numbers. They were much more difficult targets to hit, and were faster than either the St-Chamond or Schneider. The German artillery was seldom available in large enough numbers, and so single gun sites could be attacked by several tanks at once. A German soldier wrote of his unit's encounter with American Renaults near St-Mihiel: "Fleets of small tanks, each armed with a single gun or machine-gun, appeared with the rapidity of weasels in and behind our gun positions with this weird rabble spewing up like the spawn of hell." In the early autumn of 1918 some German units began introducing tactical changes which stressed the need to mass anti-tank equipment into defensive clusters, the aim being to prevent the larger number of tanks from picking off isolated gun sites one by one. This practice never became widespread enough to have much effect. Instead, the light tanks became more numerous and dangerous.

Anti-tank rifles did not prove to be a major threat to the Renault, although they could penetrate armor at close ranges. It was generally found that the polygonal turret was less vulnerable to the AT rifles than the round Girod turrets as the integrity of the flat armor plate was higher. However, mines were a serious problem for the small Renaults and could easily blow a tank apart. Mines were usually of an improvised nature, and not used in large enough numbers to have

A Renault FT *char signal* of the 505e Regiment moves forward past accompanying US infantry near Limey in the Meurthe region on October 14, 1918. These tanks often had a canvas tarp over parts of the superstructure in the hopes of preventing rain damage to the delicate radio transmitter. (NARA)

much effect on tank combat, destroying only 13 Renaults during the war. So far as is known no French tanks ever encountered a German tank in combat, in no small measure due to the very small number of German tanks.

The other main enemy of the Renault tank was the anti-tank trench; far more Renaults were put out of action temporarily by trenches than by any enemy weapon. The Renaults were simply too small to cross the wider ditches. Large shell-holes also posed a real problem. The French tried to overcome this with both tactical and technical solutions. Renault units were not supposed to be committed to overcome a trench system without supporting engineer troops or specially trained infantry. The infantry or sappers were supposed to break down the trench walls with shovels at a few points to permit passage, but this seldom happened in practice. The technical solution was the use of bridging tanks. In the later months of the war, the Renault units were scheduled to receive a special support version of the Renault tank, armed with a 75mm BS "*petoire*" short howitzer. This support tank was also fitted with attachment points to permit it to carry a small bridge on the front which could be laid over anti-tank ditches. The war ended before this program could be put into action.

Mechanical problems stopped more Renaults than any other cause bar trenches. The fan-belts were a constant headache right up to the end of the war. In one action, an American Renault FT company used up more than one new fan-belt per tank in less than a day. The problems were caused both by the poor quality of the belts and by driver inexperience; the belts could be broken if the engine were suddenly revved up too fast, or could snap after a cold start. After prolonged use, they tended to swell and begin to slip. This was an all-too-frequent occurrence which led to even more serious problems: if slipping went unnoticed by the driver, the engine overheated, the engine cylinders jammed or the piston rod broke, and eventually the crank-case could be split. No technical solution for the problem was found during the

Landmines were a novel hazard in tank warfare in 1918, as seen in the case of this American Renault FT *char canon* with the Girod turret, disabled during the Ardennes battles on October 12, 1918, near Fléville. (NARA)

war aside from careful driver training and frequent belt replacement. The dire consequences of this seemingly minor problem highlight the basic immaturity of the automotive technology on which the early tank was based, as well as the exhausted state of the French war industries.

By the late summer of 1918 the Renault FT was finally becoming available in large numbers. By August over 2,000 had been delivered, and the pace of production was increasing. Two more regiments were formed in June, and one each in July and August. By September there were 21 French and two American FT battalions. The American battalions were supposed to be equipped with US-manufactured light tanks. These were not yet available, and so the French Army agreed to provide equipment for three light tank battalions. The initial commander of the US tank battalions was LtCol George S. Patton. Interestingly enough, the commander of the tank training center in the United States was another officer who would become famous in the Second World War – LtCol Dwight Eisenhower. The Renaults were involved in ten battles after the Soissons offensive, usually at company or battalion strength. The next major deployment came on August 28, 1918, when seven battalions from the 502e, 503e and 505e Regiments were used to support the French Tenth Army around Crécy-au Mont/Crouy during five savage days of fighting. Coinciding with British actions in Flanders, the fighting pushed the Germans back from the last scraps of territory won during the Ludendorff offensive.

**F**  **ST-CHAMOND, GROUPEMENT XIII, 1918**

The third and final production batch of the St-Chamond with the angled roof and M1897 75mm gun had a much simpler paint scheme than that used on earlier tanks of this type which was applied at the factory rather than in the field. It consisted of large patterns of the standard colors of ochre, brown and green over artillery gray. From photos, it would appear that the patterns were similar, but not standardized. The vehicle production number was usually painted on the tanks in white. By this stage of the war, unit insignia tended to be much more restrained than during the early combats.

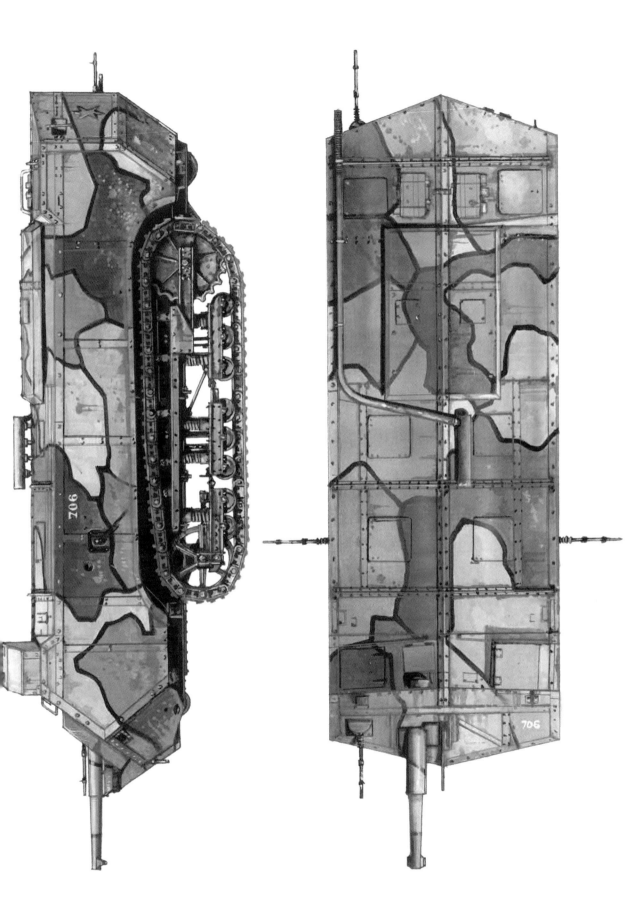

What was significant about the summer fighting was not so much the territory regained as the changing tactics. The stalemate of the trenches was finally ending. Machine-gun nests could be readily eliminated by the tanks, permitting the infantry to advance for distances that would have been unimaginable in 1916 or 1917. The attacks were not necessarily preceded by heavy artillery bombardment, since the resulting craters hindered the passage of tanks.

The new American 344th and 345th Battalions were first blooded in the fighting near St-Mihiel on September 12, 1918. Their real trial-by-fire came later in the month during the Meuse–Argonne Forest battles which began on September 26 and dragged on through November 1, 1918. The American tank battalions were supported by three French tank battalions, making this operation one of the largest involving the Renault FT during the war. The US Army received 514 Renault FTs during the course of the war but the American tank production program never had any impact on the fighting due to persistent delays. Four Renaults and a set of plans were shipped to the US in 1917, but the plans had to be converted from their metric measurements in order to allow use of US machine tools. In addition, the early versions of the Renaults shipped to the US were virtually hand-built, with many small variations in design. Not all of the bugs had been worked out on the Renault, and so there was a constant stream of changes coming from the French factories. The American-built Renault, codenamed the "six-Ton Special Tractor," differed in many small details from the French original. The Renault 18CV engine proved impossible for US firms, and so a Buda engine was adopted in its place.

The US government ordered 4,440 "six-Ton Tanks Model 1917" from three assembly plants: the Van Dorn Iron Works, Maxwell Motor Company and C. L. Best Tractor Company. The first tank was not completed at the Van Dorn Iron Works until October 1918, and 64 were finished by the end of the war. Ten had been shipped to France and arrived before the Armistice, but not in time to see any fighting. By the end of 1918, 209 had been completed,

A column of Renault FT led by a *char canon* of AS 337, 13e BCL, 505e Regiment, while moving forward to support the AEF 80th Division in the Argonne fighting near Rampont on October 10, 1918. (NARA)

**Major French tank actions, 1917–18**

| | Battle | Tank units | Schneider | St-Chamond | Renault FT |
|---|---|---|---|---|---|
| **1917** | | | | | |
| April 16 | Chemin-des-Dames | 10 Schneider groups | 132 | | |
| May 5 | Moulin-de-Laffaux | 2 Schneider, 1 St-Chamond groups | 31 | 16 | |
| October 23 | Malmaison | 3 Schneider, 2 St-Chamond groups | 41 | 32 | |
| **1918** | | | | | |
| May 28 | Cantigny | 3 Schneider batteries | ~12 | | |
| May 31 | Ploisy-Chazelle | 3 FT battalions | | | ~220 |
| June 2 | Faverolles-Corcy | 1 FT battalion | | | ~70 |
| June 11 | Matz valley | 2 Schneider, 2 St-Chamond *groupements* | 75 | 103 | |
| June 28 | Cutry-St-Pierre | 4 FT companies | | | 60 |
| July 9 | Porte and Loges farm | 4 Schneider batteries | ~15 | | |
| July 18 | Soissons | 3 Schneider, 4 St-Chamond *groupements*; 6 FT battalions | 123 | 96 | 255 |
| August 10 | Ressons-sur-Matz | 1 FT battalion | | | 30 |
| August 16 | Tillaloy | 3 Schneider groups | 32 | | |
| August 17 | Roye | 1 FT battalion | | | 45 |
| August 20 | Oise-Aisne | 1 Schneider group, 1 St-Chamond group, 1 FT battalion | 12 | 28 | 30 |
| August 28 | Crécy-au-Mont/Crouy | 7 FT battalions | | | 305 |
| September 12 | St-Mihiel | 2 Schneider, 2 St-Chamond groups; 3 FT battalions; 2 US FT battalions | 24 | 36 | 309 |
| September 14 | Thielt-Gand | 1 St-Chamond *groupement* | | ~40 | |
| September 14 | Colombe farm | 3 FT battalions | | | 85 |
| September 26 | Champagne | 3 Schneider, 2 St-Chamond groups, 7 FT battalions | 34 | 27 | 330 |
| September 26 | Argonne forest | 2 Schneider, 2 St-Chamond groups, 4 FT battalions, 2 US FT battalions | 22 | ~20 | 355 |
| October 17 | Petit Verley | 1 FT battalion | | | 69 |
| October 25 | Guise | 3 FT battalions | | | ~200 |
| October 25 | Hunding-Stellung | 3 FT battalions | | | ~200 |
| October 31 | Escaut advance | 2 FT battalions | | | ~150 |

**Heavy tanks deployed, 1917–18**

| | Schneider | St-Chamond |
|---|---|---|
| 31 March, 1917 | 208 | 48 |
| 21 March, 1918 | 245 | 222 |
| 1 August, 1918 | 51 | 40 |
| 1 September, 1918 | 40 | 36 |
| 1 October, 1918 | 60 | 40 |
| 1 November, 1918 | 51 | 54 |

**French tank combat engagements, 1917–18**

| | Schneider | St-Chamond | Renault FT | Total |
|---|---|---|---|---|
| 1917 | 175 | 41 | 0 | 216 |
| 1918 | 473 | 375 | 3,140 | 3,988 |
| Total | 648 | 416 | 3,292* | 4,356 |

*includes US Renault FT engagements*

and it was decided to finish a total of 950 tanks based on the supply of finished parts and other material on hand when the war ended. These were completed in 1919 and formed the bulk of the US Army's tank force well into the 1930s along with 213 Renault FTs brought back from France.

Italy had received three FTs in June 1918, but the French were unable and unwilling to provide enough to form combat units. Plans to build the Renault FT in Italy were cut short by the end of the war. After the war Italy embarked on its own light tank, the Fiat 3000, which was derived from the FT.

## THE FINAL OFFENSIVE

On September 26, 1918, seven Renault battalions began operations in Flanders and Champagne as part of the final Allied offensive. The September–October fighting was marked by wretched weather and determined German resistance from heavily fortified positions. Nevertheless, machine-guns and artillery alone were no longer a guarantee against a determined infantry attack if bolstered by tanks. Three more regiments, totaling a further nine battalions, were committed later in the month on other fronts as part of the general offensive. The actions of the French tank battalions have attracted little historical attention. In the 1920s and 1930s, the advocates of mechanization ignored these encounters as mere examples of primitive infantry support tactics. They did not fit into the grand dream of sweeping offensives by massed formations of tanks with deep breakthroughs.

Judged by the high standards of the tank enthusiasts like Estienne and his British counterparts, the French tank actions in 1918 were not particularly impressive. However, the dreams of the tank pioneers were unrealistic given

The American-manufactured Renault copy, the Six-Ton Tank, had a number of structural differences from its ancestor and is most easily distinguished by the presence of the muffler on the left side. This example, pictured in 1927, is from the US Marine Corps Light Tank Platoon, East Coast Expeditionary Force, and is being unloaded in China during the turmoil in Shanghai. (NARA)

the primitive state of the equipment available in 1918. The little Renaults were not really capable of any prolonged operations; after a few days of fighting, they were mechanically exhausted. Few units had more than half their strength after a couple of days of hard fighting and, inevitably, a fair percentage of tanks were stuck in trenches and shell craters. The Renaults had a maximum range of only about 25 miles before refueling, and refueling was a very cumbersome adventure in heavily shelled areas since lorries could not reach the tanks. Fuel had to be brought up on sledges towed behind tanks.

Judged by more realistic standards, the Renault units had accomplished their task. The French Army, which had been nearly as badly broken in the spring of 1917 as had the Russian Army, was rejuvenated and returned to the fight. While the credit for this can hardly be given to the Renault alone, the availability of large numbers of light tanks was an enormous morale-booster for the weary infantry: the *poilus* no longer faced the machine-guns alone. Instead, they could advance behind the cover of the little tanks, watching as their nemesis, the machine-gun nest, was smashed and overrun by the tank. There were no grand drives in 1918 for the Renaults, only a monotonous string of brutish little engagements between Renaults and German defensive positions. These skirmishes may not have represented the birth of blitzkrieg, but they certainly heralded the end of trench warfare.

## PLAN 1919

The Schneider CA, St-Chamond, and Renault FT were the only three French tank types to see combat, but plans were under way for other designs, especially new heavy tanks. As mentioned earlier, Schneider had been working

The FCM 1A was the most futuristic tank developed by France during the war, with a turret-mounted 105mm howitzer, 35mm armor and a 40 tonne weight. Although favored by the armaments ministry, it was rejected by Clémenceau and Estienne who preferred its monstrous offspring, the gigantic FCM *Char* 2C. (NARA)

The ultimate French World War I tank was the monstrous FCM *Char* 2C breakthrough tank. Although intended for the spring 1919 offensive, production was delayed into 1921. In May 1940, the six operational tanks of the 51e BCC were lost to a Stuka attack when their transport train was hit near the Meuse-sur-Meuse station. (Patton Museum)

on an evolutionary follow-on design that eventually petered out with the advent of the Renault FT. However, there was still a desire for a larger tank. A heavy tank had been commissioned by the DSA in July 1916 from the FCM (*Forges et Chantiers de la Méditerranée*) at its La Seyne shipyard. The FCM heavy tank weighed 40 tonnes, and was fitted with a 105mm howitzer in a turret; armor was 35mm, almost triple the existing standard. A preliminary design was completed in October and a full-scale wooden prototype in December 1916.

The preliminary design for the FCM A was presented to a committee including Gen Estienne on January 17, 1917, but no consensus could be reached regarding electric versus mechanical transmissions, and Estienne preferred a rapid-fire 75mm gun. The tank was powered by a 200hp Renault engine, but Renault was already over-committed to engine manufacture for the aircraft industry. As a result, a decision was held off until the first prototype, the FCM 1A, was completed. Trials of the prototype began on December 10, 1917, and were generally satisfactory. A range of variants were discussed including the heavier *Char* 1B, weighing 45 tonnes.

FCM had also studied a *char lourd de rupture* (heavy breakthrough tank) designated the 2C that was significantly longer and therefore more suitable for crossing the widened German trenches. Loucheur and the armaments ministry favored the smaller and more practical 40-tonne *Char* 1A while war minister Georges Clémenceau and Estienne favored the larger 65-tonne *Char* 2C.

As an alternative, St-Chamond offered to manufacture a rhomboid copied from the British pattern (*char d'assaut à chénilles enveloppantes*: enclosed-track assault tank) but with a 75mm gun in the bow and four machine-gun stations in the sponsons. This never progressed beyond the paper stage. Estienne preferred the newer British designs and especially favored the Anglo-American Mark VIII Liberty tank, also known as the International. This 38-tonne tank was so large and heavy that the scheme was to manufacture the main components in Britain and the USA and then ship the parts to an assembly plant at Neuvy-Pailloux where they would be put together by imported Chinese laborers.

Estienne estimated that at least a dozen, but more likely 18, heavy tanks would be needed per division to make up for attrition; this suggested an objective of 700 heavy tanks for 40 divisions by early 1919. Pétain suggested that purchasing the Anglo-American Liberty tank would be a prudent choice, and considering that French industry would be hard-pressed to build 300 of the *Char* 2C, he suggested in a February 1918 letter that 600 Liberty tanks be ordered in parallel to the *Char* 2C. Clémenceau authorized an order for 900 to be delivered by March 1919 with plans to form 54 Liberty groups with 15 tanks each.

With the supply of Schneider and St-Chamond tanks dwindling and the prospects for other new tanks a year away, Loucheur discussed acquiring British tanks with his British counterpart, Winston Churchill, in early 1918. Churchill promised that the first 15 of 200 Mark V tanks could be delivered in March 1918 and that the British Army would like to start receiving the Renault FT in exchange. This deal quickly fell apart due to delivery delays with the new Mark V and when the British offered to substitute the Mark IV, Estienne turned down the offer as unacceptable. In the meantime, FCM was given a contract on February 21, 1918, to build the *Char* 2C even though a prototype had not even been constructed. Clémenceau wanted 300 *Char* 2C by March 1919 but Loucheur retorted that French industry was so overstretched that it would be difficult to deliver even 60. A bitter argument ensued which dragged on through most of the spring and summer.

The French heavy tank effort eventually collapsed. The British delivered 77 Mark V*s by early October 1918 and about a dozen more after the war; the remainder of the order was cancelled. These were used to convert

The Renault FT remained in French service in dwindling numbers after the war, seeing some limited combat service in the 1940 campaign. Curiously enough, this Renault FT was knocked out in the Chemin-des-Dames area in June 1940 – the very place where French tanks had seen their combat debut two decades earlier. (NARA)

Schneider and St-Chamond groups that were out of tanks but the French Mark V* units never took part in combat due to the late delivery of the tanks and problems with spare parts. They served with the 551e *Régiment de Chars de Combat* in the 1920s. The Liberty tank program was badly delayed and France cancelled its order at the end of the war before receiving any tanks. The FCM order for the *Char* 2C was slashed to ten at the end of the war and these were delivered in 1921. Curiously enough, the original Chenu powerplants were replaced by German Maybach and Daimler-Benz zeppelin engines which had been acquired as war reparations.

Besides the heavy tank programs, a number of light tank programs were also under way to supplement the Renault FT in 1919. Peugeot designed a small tank resembling the Renault FT but with a fixed superstructure and short 75mm gun; it was tested in April 1918 but none were ordered. Gen Estienne wanted to acquire 2,000 American-built Ford Three-Ton Tanks but only a handful arrived in September 1918 for trials and none saw combat. By the end of the war, a total of 3,177 Renault FTs had been manufactured, of which about 1,950 came from Renault. After the war Renault completed over 570 tanks, and total production was about 4,400 tanks from all plants (not counting American production). The Renault proved to be a staple of French arms exports after the war. It also saw more combat use in the inter-war years than any other tank. Its small size made it ideally suitable for shipment to distant lands, and its simple construction served it well even in primitive conditions.

Spain used six Schneider CA tanks in the Rif war in Morocco in the early 1920s, and the type also saw limited combat in the Spanish Civil War in 1936–37. The Renault FT tanks saw combat in Russia in 1918–20, in the Russo-Polish war of 1920, in China in the 1920s, and with French and Spanish armies in the Rif war in Morocco in the 1920s. Renault FT tanks were used in a dwindling number of campaigns in World War II, including Poland in 1939, the Battle of France in 1940, and by German troops in France in 1944. The last known combat action by the Renault FT was Afghanistan in the 1980s where a handful of tanks were used as static pillboxes or roadblocks.

**G**

### 1. RENAULT FT, 506E RAS, 1918

The Renault FT were typically painted at the factory in army green and had simple camouflage schemes that suggests they may have been painted at the factory or *en masse* in depots before being issued. The scheme usually consisted of large blotches of ochre and brown over the army green with swathes of black to hide view slits. The army serial numbers in white on the lower frame were issued in blocks to the various plants with Renault using numbers in the 66000–68000 range, Schneider (Somua) in the 69000 range, Delauney-Belleville in the 70000 range and Berliet in the 73000 range. Some of the manufacturers painted their own serial numbers on the left hull side under the turret. This is a typical Berliet example in the 2001–2801 range.

The Renault FT light battalions were organized differently from heavy tank groups, so they used the playing-card symbols in the usual fashion to identify sections rather than batteries: Spade (1), Heart (2), Diamond (3), Club (echelon). These were painted in black on a white geometric shape which identified the company: Circle (1); Square (2), Triangle (3). The markings here indicate that the tank is from the echelon section, 2nd Company.

### 2. RENAULT FT, 505E RAS, 1918

This is a typical example of a tank built by Schneider's Somua plant with the serial number (3259) from the range 3001–3601. The army serial number on the suspension frame would be in the 69000 range but is obscured by dirt. The marking on the hull rear identifies this as a tank from the 2nd Section, 1st Company.

1

2

The Renault FT remained in French service in the colonies and there were over 300 still in service in North Africa in 1940. They saw sporadic combat in 1941–42 in Syria and North Africa, these examples taking part in skirmishes with the US Army near Safi after the Operation *Torch* landings in Morocco in November 1942. (NARA)

# FURTHER READING

Coverage of the French Army in the Great War is not especially abundant in English, so it is not surprising that coverage of French tanks is so scarce. While there has been very little written in English since the classic *The Fighting Tanks* in 1933, there is an ample selection of French-language accounts.

## Unpublished documents

Jeffrey Clarke, *Military Technology in Republican France: The Evolution of the French Armored Force 1917–1940* (doctoral dissertation, Duke University, 1969)

BrigGen S. D. Rockenbach, *Operations of the Tank Corps AEF with the 1st American Army Sept. 18 to November 1918* (US Army, 1918)

## Articles

Boisloup, D. V., "Les unités de chars moyens 1916–1918", *De Bello*, No. 4 (1978), pp. 10–18.

Boisloup, D. V., "Les unités de chars légers 1917–1918", *De Bello*, No. 9 (1979), pp. 18–23.

Buffetaut, Yves, "Les chars français a la Malmaison", *Steelmasters*, No. 33 (Jun–Jul 1999), pp. 45–49.

Buffetaut, Yves, "Les chars Schneider au Chemin-des-Dames 16 avril 1917", *Steelmasters*, No. 19 (Feb–Mar 1997), pp. 50–55.

Danjou, Pascal, "Le char Schneider CA1", *Minitracks*, No. 8 (2008), pp. 8–17.

Danjou, Pascal, "Les Mark V* de l'Armée française", *Minitracks*, No. 6 (2007), pp. 8–13.

Greenhalgh, Elizabeth, "Technology Development in Coalition: The Case of the First World War Tank", *International History Review*, December 2000, pp. 757–1008.

Micheletti, Eric, "Berry-au-Bac 16 avril 1917 à 6h30: La première attaque des chars d'assaut français", *Gazette des Armes*, No. 116, April 1983, pp. 37–42.

Pesqueur, M., "1917: Berry-au-Bac: Baptême du feu pour les chars français", *Batailles & Blindés*, No. 13 (Mar–Apr 2006), pp. 64–79.

Vauvillier, François, "Renault ou la seconde naissance du char", *Tank Zone*, Aug–Sep 2009, pp.26–37.

Vauvillier, François, "Et vint le Schneider: Brillié, Estienne et la chenille Holt", *Tank Zone*, Dec–Jan 2008/09, pp. 20–31.

Vauvillier, François, 'Saint-Chamond, le beau monster rate de la section technique", *Tank Zone*, Apr–May 2009, pp. 24–36.

Vauvillier, François, "L'aube du char en France: L'idée de l'engin du no man's land avant Estienne", *Tank Zone*, Aug–Sep 2009, pp. 26–37.

Vauvillier, François, "Des tracteurs a chenilles pour l'artillerie 1: Les caterpillars remourqueurs Holt, Baby Holt et Schneider CD", *Guerre, Blindés & Matériel*, No. 86, 2009, pp. 54–63.

## Books

Buffetaut, Yves and Bruno Jurkiewicz, *Magin sauve Paris 11 Juni 1918, La bataille du Matz* (Ysec: 2001)

Danjou, Pascal, *Renault FT* (Trackstory: 2009)

Dutil, Léon, *Les chars d'assaut: Leur création et leur rôle pendant la guerre 1915–1918* (Berger-Levrault: 1919)

Duvignac, André, *Histoire de l'armée motorisée* (Imp. Nationale: 1947)

Gougaud, Alain, *L'aube de la gloire: Les auto-mitrailleuses et les chars français pendant la grande guerre* (Musée des Blindés: 1987)

Guenaff, Didier and Bruno Jurkiewicz, *Les Chars de la Victoire 1918* (Ysec: 2004)

Hatry, Gilbert, *Renault: Usine de guerre 1914–1918* (Lafourcade: 1978)

Jeudy, Jean-Gabriel, *Chars de France* (ETAI: 1997)

Jones, Ralph, G. Rarey and R. J. Icks, *The Fighting Tanks from 1916 to 1933* (National Service Press: 1933)

Jurkiewicz, Bruno, *Les chars français au combat 1917–1918* (ECPAD/Ysec: 2008)

Kolomiets, Maksim and Semyon Fiedosiyev, *Renault FT* (Wyd. Militaria: 2005)

Laroussinie, Roger, *Méchanique de la Victoire: La grande histoire des chars d'assaut* (Albin Michel: 1972)

Lafitte, R., *L'artillerie d'assaut de 1916 à 1918* (Lavauzelle: 1921)

Lawrynowicz, Witold, *Renault FT* (Progres: 2006)

Lawrynowicz, Witold, *Schneider CA–St-Chamond* (AJ Press: 2008)

Mayet, Jean, *Le Char 2C*, (Musée des Blindés: 1996)

Ortholan, Henri, *La guerre des chars 1916–1918* (Bernard Giovangeli: 2007).

Perré, J., *Batailles et combats des chars français: L'année d'apprentissage 1917* (Lavauzelle: 1937)

Perré, J., *Batailles et combats des chars français: La bataille defensive avril–juillet 1918* (Lavauzelle: 1940)

Ramspacher, E. G., et. al., *Chars et blindés français* (Lavauzelle: 1979)

Ramspacher, E. G., *Le Général Estienne: Père des chars* (Lavauzelle: 1983)

Touzin, Pierre, *Les véhicules blindés français 1900–1944* (EPA: 1979)

Touzin, Pierre and Christian Gurtner, *Armour in Profile Number 13: Renault FT* (Profile Publications: 1967).

Zaloga, Steven, *Vanguard 46: The Renault FT Light Tank* (Osprey Publishing: 1988)

# INDEX

Numbers in bold refer to plates and illustrations.